Hc

Kasia Reay

Illustrated by Selina Rayner

Schofield&Sims

This is Yaz. She has lots of curls in her dark hair.

This is Zack. His hair is short and fair.

This is Nish. Her hair is long
and dark.

This is Jess. Her hair loops and
coils all down her back.

This is Zaid. His hair was longer and thicker, but he had it cut.

This is Viv. Her hair is getting wetter and wetter.

This is Tom. All his hair is on his chin. It is a beard!